LIGHTS AT CHICKASAW POINT & THE TWO GARCONS

AMERICAN CHAPTERS

GRETA GORSUCH

WAYZGOOSE PRESS

.

Book design and editing by Maggie Sokolik, Wayzgoose Press

Cover Design by DJ Rogers, Book Branders

CONTENTS

LIGHTS AT CHICKASAW POINT

THE TWO GARCONS

FROM THE AUTHOR

Welcome to *American Chapters!*

The *American Chapters* series presents short stories in vivid and easy-to-read 500-word chapters, perfect for English language learners internationally and adult literacy learners in countries where English is commonly used.

All *American Chapters* print stories are also offered as audiobooks for learners who want to hear and read the stories, and hear the sounds of American English.

American Chapters are lively, relevant, and realistic short stories about living in the United States of America. About Americans, immigrants, sojourners, and the diverse peoples living in this wide landscape, the stories touch on the tough questions and the great things in life—things like work, ethnic differences, our connections to the past, our place in nature, being new, small town life, personal loss, and above all, new beginnings.

LIGHTS AT CHICKASAW POINT

CHAPTER ONE

There was a knock on the door. Brian Longfield, the campground host, looked up from his newspaper. It was 7:30 a.m. Brian was drinking his tea, reading the newspaper, and looking out the window, all at the same time. There was another knock. "Hello? Helloooo?" came a high voice. "Is this the campground host? Are you in there?"

Brian got up and opened the trailer door. Outside was an old man, wearing a very old hat. He looked up at Brian in the doorway. His little blue eyes were even smaller behind thick glasses. "Yes," said Brian. "I'm the campground host. I'm on after eight this morning. Is there something wrong?"

The old man said, "Oh. Well, can you come now? I'm in Number 23."

Brian didn't say anything. The old man waited.

Then Brian said, "What's the problem, then?" He came out of his trailer and shut the door behind him. He came down the stairs. With the old man following him, he walked to the back of his trailer. He had his tools there.

The whole time, the old man talked about the problem he was having with his camper van. He took his hat off. Then he put his hat back on. Then he did the same with his thick glasses. There was something wrong with the lights. They wouldn't turn on. And maybe there was something wrong with the water at Number 23.

Brian listened. Sometimes he said, "Uh-huh," to show he was listening. The two men walked to Number 23. It was a beautiful morning to walk through the park. The park had a lake. There were thirty campsites by the lake. Each campsite had a number. Brian's trailer was " Number 1." This was the campsite for the campground host. Then the numbers went up as you walked west on the campground road. There was Number 2, and then Number 3, and so on. Number 23 was a little far from Brian's campsite. But that was OK. Brian liked being a campground host because he liked to walk. He liked lakes and trees. And parks like his park, Trace Park, had a lake, and lots and lots of trees.

Each campsite had electricity and water. If you had a trailer, or a camper van, you could have lights. Some trailers had a sink and shower. And some trailers had a TV and a refrigerator. It was like being in a small home. The best part was that you could sit by a beautiful lake. The park could be quiet. Campers at the park could wake up to the sound of birds.

Brian and the old man got to Number 23. This was a large, expensive trailer. It was older. You could tell it was out in the wind and rain for many years. But at one time, this was one of the best trailers you could buy.

The old man was still talking. He said, "I can't turn on the lights at all." They went inside the trailer, and he showed Brian the lights. They were dead.

Brian went back outside and looked at the electricity for Number 23. Then he did a few things. From inside the trailer, the old man called, "Oh, the lights are on!"

"OK," said Brian. "What else?" Then they checked the water at Number 23. Brian pointed at something and said, "I can't repair this. You need to call a trailer repair service."

"Oh," said the man. His face fell. "Do you know anyone? Someone cheap?"

Brian understood that the old man didn't have the money for a trailer repairman to come. There were probably a lot of small things wrong with his trailer. Now it was the big things going wrong. Electricity and water were big things. Brian said, "Well, maybe I can try something."

The old man brightened up. He nodded.

CHAPTER TWO

Brian walked back to his trailer. It was 9:30 now. The sun was higher up in the sky. It was getting warmer. It was only February in Trace Park. But, Trace Park was just outside of Belden, Mississippi. Mississippi was in the southern U.S. It did get cold in winter. But most of the time it was very warm compared to Minnesota or New York or Indiana. In those states, it snowed. In Mississippi, it rained.

Mr. Felton, the old man in Number 23, kept saying how helpful Brian was. "This makes a big difference to me," he said in his high old man's voice.

Brian said, "You really need to have a trailer repair service for that. My repair will only last a few days. As long as you understand that."

Mr. Felton nodded. Brian sighed. He was sure he would be at Number 23 again soon.

Brian enjoyed the walk back to Number 1. He enjoyed the lake on his left, and the trailers and camper vans on the right. The Lakeside Campground was not full. There were only about seven campsites being used. It was February. The rangers at Trace Park called February the "off season." Their busiest time was June, July, and August when large family groups came to Trace Park to camp.

The campers at the park now were not large family groups. Mostly they were old people. They were quiet. They stayed for a long time. They only had to pay $200 per month to stay at the park during the off season. They got a "senior citizen" discount. They didn't have to pay extra for electricity or water. So Brian was happy. His job was easy in some ways.

Large family groups in the summer months were sometimes hard on campground hosts. Everyone was on vacation. School was out. If the kids made noise, the campground host had to stop them. Moms and dads did not like that, sometimes.

Summer people also liked to drink. Sometimes that made for trouble. And yes, campground hosts had to speak to the drinkers, too. Sometimes the park rangers had to come. A ranger might tell them, "Your kids are watching us, you know. Do you want them to see you drinking and loud like this?" That sometimes stopped it.

But Brian soon learned that the "winter people," the senior citizens, had their own problems. They didn't have any money. And that was the reason they came to Trace Park. They came in their old trailers and lived in them. This meant that Brian had a lot of repairs to do.

It was cold in their home states. One older woman at Number

14 told Brian she was from Minnesota. She couldn't pay for heat during the winter. She couldn't move the snow in front of her house. So she had another person live in her house, for money.

Once a week, Brian could see three or four campers get into one car and drive into town for groceries. They shared the cost of food, and the gas for their car. Food was much cheaper in Mississippi.

Some of the winter campers also had health problems. They were old, of course. The warm weather was easier on them. In Mississippi, they wouldn't fall on snow or ice, and hurt themselves. There was a doctor in Pontotoc that the winter campers went to. Pontotoc was a small town 10 minutes away. The doctor was good. But the main thing was that he didn't cost very much. He was kind to them. He listened to them.

Brian didn't have to talk to the winter people to understand these things. He knew about them very well. Brian was a lot like them. He had little money. His trailer was only five years old. But he couldn't buy another trailer if he wanted to. He couldn't pay for any big repairs. The only way Brian could live was to be a campground host. He could stay at the park free. This was lucky. If he wasn't a campground host, he could not take care of his wife, Nancy. And she needed care. That cost money.

CHAPTER THREE

Brian sat down again to his newspaper. After he finished a second cup of tea, there was a knock on his door. He sighed. Who was it this time?

He opened the door and saw Ranger Jack Madison. Ranger Madison was the youngest of five rangers at Trace Park. He was only 30. He was very good at talking to large family groups and drinkers during the summer. Brian was 30 years older than Jack, but they got on well. They both liked to repair things. They both liked the lake and the trees. For some repairs, Brian would borrow tools from Jack. For other kinds of repairs, Jack would borrow Brian's tools.

Brian got some tea for Ranger Madison and they sat outside. "What's up?" asked Brian. He knew Ranger Madison worked nights. Even in the winter, one park ranger had to drive around the park the night. This was to make sure the campers were OK. Trace Park also had a lot of animals. You could see deer, turkeys, and ducks on any day. Trace Park was off-limits to hunters. You could not hunt animals in the park. But that did not stop some hard sorts of men. They liked guns, and they liked hunting. Sometimes they came into the park at night, and hunted whatever animal they could. The night ranger had to stop anyone who tried to do that.

Jack Madison looked tired, but he enjoyed the tea. He said, "There's been someone over at Chickasaw Point. Do you know where that is?" He pointed to the west along the lake.

Brian could see it. It was another campground. But it was closed during the winter. Trace Park didn't have enough campers to keep it open. After dark, it was just a black forest.

"Really?" asked Brian. "How do they get in?" The Chickasaw Point Campground was closed, and the road was blocked.

"Oh, I guess they park their car and then walk in," said Ranger Madison. "Anyway, keep an eye out. There are lights right at sunset. And at night. At least that's what a few campers told us. We want to make sure there aren't any hunters. Or maybe it's kids. But they shouldn't be out there after dark. It's such a lonely, dark place. It's deep forest. They could get hurt."

"OK," said Brian. "I'll keep an eye out. I'll call the park office if I see anything."

"Yeah," said Jack Madison. "Someone should be there at the office. If there isn't any answer just leave a message. Don't go out there yourself. Some of those hunters are hard men. They don't care about anything."

Ranger Madison thanked Brian for the tea. He drove away in his park car.

As Brian watched him, he saw an older lady from Number 6 come out of her camper van. She walked over to see him. When she got close enough, he said, "Is it your refrigerator again?"

"Yes," said Mrs. Poe. "I'm sorry but could you look at it again? I have all my groceries in there." It was like this every day. With Mrs. Poe, it was her refrigerator. Or sometimes her toilet. Other campers had other problems. Their trailers were old, and in bad repair. Last week, one camper asked Brian to drive him to the doctor. "Sorry," said Brian. "I don't repair people."

Brian sighed. Then he said, "I'll be there in a few minutes."

CHAPTER FOUR

Brian went to Pontotoc to have lunch. He got a few hamburgers with tea. He took them to Nancy's nursing home. Maybe she would be hungry.

Brian's wife Nancy no longer spoke. She was 54. She knew him sometimes. But, sometimes she did not. She stopped speaking last month. Before that, she couldn't remember things. She forgot when she ate, and said she was hungry. But she had lunch only ten minutes before. Brian once found her in their truck. She forgot her keys. And she forgot the word "keys." When

Brian gave her the keys, she asked "What are these for? Are we going somewhere?"

Nancy worked in an office. When her memory started to go, Brian got a call from Nancy's boss. She was upset. She said, "I really like Nancy. But is something wrong with her? No one can work with her. She doesn't answer questions. And she never says 'hello'. This morning she was two hours late. She couldn't tell me why. When I pointed at the clock to show it was 10 AM, she asked me what the clock was for."

The boss was sorry, but this could not go on. Something was wrong.

Nancy had to leave work. But this was truly bad luck. Brian didn't have a regular job. He made money building houses. He repaired things for people. He had a gift. He could repair cars, refrigerators, washing machines, and just about anything else. But even gifted repairmen didn't have regular work. Some days he would work, and some days he would not. Without Nancy's job, he could not pay for a doctor.

Nancy's doctor told him that she could not be left alone at home. The doctor asked, "Is there someone who can stay with her?"

Brian shook his head. "We never had kids. Nancy has a sister. But she's helping out her own kids. And she's 200 miles away."

The doctor looked sad. Then she said, "Then your wife needs to be in a nursing home. She can't be left alone."

Brian just sat there. They didn't have the money for that.

After a month, it became clear. Without Nancy's job, Brian could not keep the house. He thought about what to do. They had a trailer, so that was a place he could live in. But if he had to live in his trailer, he had to go somewhere warm. That meant Alabama, or Mississippi, or Florida. Florida cost too much. Everyone wanted to live there. He crossed Florida off the list.

Then he found out about Trace Park in Mississippi. They

needed a campground host. He called the park, and he got the job.

Brian called Nancy's sister to tell her they were moving to Mississippi.

"MISSISSIPPI? No one goes to Mississippi," she said. "Why there?"

Brian answered, "It's where I got work." He told her about Trace Park. "There's a nursing home for Nancy. It's the best I can do. You know how our money is."

"OK," she said, quietly. "I'll try to visit in March. My kids are off school then. Maybe I can bring them along?"

"Always welcome, you know that," said Brian. He liked Nancy's sister.

When Brian got to the Pontotoc Rose Nursing Home, he found Nancy in the sun room. She didn't look up. He opened the bag with the hamburgers. He picked up her hand. Then he put a hamburger in her hand.

She didn't take it. She looked out the window.

CHAPTER FIVE

When Brian got back to Trace Park, it was getting dark. The days were short in February. It would be a long, quiet night. He sat outside for a few minutes to enjoy the sunset. He heard a bird call. He heard a fish splash in the lake. He could see the dark trees of Chickasaw Point. Then he saw the light.

Ranger Madison was right. Someone was out there, in the growing darkness. The light moved slowly. It seemed to go to the lake. Then it went out. After that it was just a dark forest.

What? Who was that? Why would they go to Chickasaw

Point? Brian got out his cell phone. He called the Trace Park office. He wanted to tell the rangers. But there wasn't anyone at the office. "Please leave a message," said the telephone. Brian left a message. Then he saw the light again. It was in a different spot, but still by the lake.

Brian decided to walk over to Chickasaw Point. He would be quiet. Whoever it was wouldn't see him. He had his cell phone. He could call for help if he had to. He walked down the road to the Chickasaw Point Campground entrance. And there was a car. No, two cars. They were empty.

By this time it was full dark. Very quietly, Brian walked down the dark road to the campground. It was so dark he could not see the lake. But he knew he must be getting close. Then he heard a big SPLASH. He knew he was near the lake now.

Then he heard voices. It sounded like two or three men. Brian got a little closer. Now he could hear three men. But they weren't speaking English. He didn't know what language they were speaking. He heard a long run of words. He could hear a few English words, like "nine o'clock" and "big concert." He heard one of the men laugh softly.

Brian could just see the men. There were three. And they were... what? Fishing? Then a bird in the trees called loudly. In the silence, Brian could hear the bird fly away into the night sky.

One of the men turned his head. He asked in soft English, "Hello? Is somebody there?"

Brian stepped forward, "Hi," he said. "I saw your lights. I'm the campground host over at Lakeside."

Then one of the men turned on a small light. Brian could see three men sitting in chairs next to the lake. They *were* fishing.

The first man said, "Hello friend. We're just fishing."

A second man stood up and waved hello. He was small and dark. He smiled and said, "Just fishing here."

"Oh," said Brian. "Do the park rangers know you're here?

They're worried that someone is coming here at night. Chickasaw Point Campground is closed until May."

"Oh, dear," said the first man. He was taller. He had a friendly smile. He, too, was very dark, with large brown eyes. "Well," he said, "I'm Mohinder Singh. I'm a doctor at the North Mississippi State Hospital. Should we check with the park rangers? There's never anyone at the park office."

Brian said, "That's true. I left a message for them when I saw your lights tonight. Let me call them to tell them it's OK." He took out his cell phone to make the call. That was strange. His cell phone didn't work here. The phone came on, but the screen said: *No network.*

"Our cell phones don't work here either," said Dr. Singh.

"That's strange. I live at Lakeside Campground. The cell phone is fine there. Anyway, the rangers will get my message. I'll stay with you in case a ranger comes."

One of the men got another chair from his car. Brian sat with the men for a while. They talked quietly so the fish could not hear them. Two of the men were doctors. They were from India. They lived in Tupelo. "It's a ten minute drive only," said the second man. The third man was from Pakistan. He worked for a computer company in Tupelo. He wrote computer software. They all had young kids.

Dr. Singh said, "My wife misses good fresh fish. She can't find any at the grocery store." The Pakistani man said, "Yes, yes. But I don't eat fish. I just come with my friends to talk while they fish."

The second man, Dr. Dheram, caught a small fish. He threw it back into the lake. It was too young to take.

Then the Pakistani man caught a large fish. "Ahh!" all the men said. "Here, I give it to you. Gladly," said the Pakistani man.

After ten minutes, Brian heard someone walking to the lake from the campground road. It was Ranger Jack Madison. Brian and the men said hello. Brian told Ranger Madison what happened. He explained the men were fishing.

Ranger Madison checked to make sure they had Mississippi State fishing licenses. They did. He said to the men, "Chickasaw Point Campground is closed until spring. It's just so dark out here. And we don't know who is out here at night. I'd like you to fish at Lakeside Campground. It's open now. Brian is the campground host there. Right, Brian?"

"Right," said Brian. "There's a nice fishing spot there. I'll show it to you."

CHAPTER SIX

Ranger Madison gave Brian a ride back to Number 1 at the Lakeside Campground. "Well," he said, "That explains the lights at sundown. But someone says they also saw a light at two or three in the morning."

"I wonder who it is?" said Brian. "Two o'clock in the morning is a strange time to fish."

"Yes, and that worries me. Please just call the office. Even if you have to leave a message, it's OK. I'll check out Chickasaw

Point. No need for you to go. We don't know who is out there," said Ranger Madison.

"OK," said Brian. He felt a little hurt. Then he said, "By the way, my cell phone doesn't work out on Chickasaw Point. Do you know anything about it?"

"Right. I've heard that. No one's phone works out there. I called the telephone people about it. They have no idea why there's no cell phone service out there. It's always been that way."

"Hmmmm. Well, OK. See you later," said Brian. Jack Madison waved and drove away into the night.

A few hours later Brian's cell phone rang. He was half asleep at his table. His head nodded over his newspaper. It was Nancy's sister.

"How is Nancy?" she asked.

"No better. She doesn't talk. And I don't know if she knows if I'm there," said Brian.

"It's hard to believe," she said. Then she sighed. They were silent for a minute. "Well," she said, finally, "We'd like to come visit in March. The kids have a short school break. Would that be OK?"

"Of course. But don't expect much from Nancy," said Brian. "I'll find you a motel out near Trace Park."

"Sure enough. I'll call you when I know the dates," she said. They hung up.

That night he dreamed of Nancy. She was talking, but he couldn't hear anything she said. Her mouth moved, but no sound came out. In his dream, he said, "I can't hear you, honey. What is it?"

The dream-Nancy held up her hand. She had something in it. It was small and dark. Some kind of stone? With a sharp point? He couldn't tell.

Then he fell into a deeper sleep, and he couldn't remember his dreams.

CHAPTER SEVEN

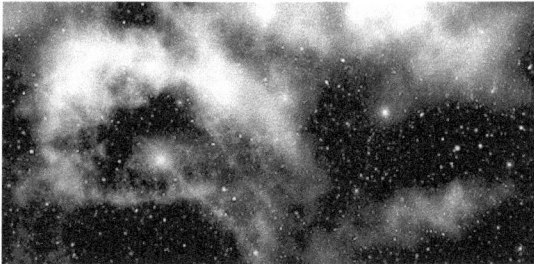

A few days went by. Campers came by and asked for help. Old Mr. Felton from Number 23 was having trouble with his lights again. He held his old hat in one hand. They stood outside his trailer. Brian said, "I can't help you any more with this. I don't know how to repair this. It's too big for me. You need to call the trailer repair service." He walked away.

Mr. Felton called after him. Brian kept walking. Later he saw a truck in front of Number 23. He could see a man and Mr. Felton talk for a long time. Finally the man went inside Mr. Felton's trailer. After an hour, Brian could see the lights go on.

Some new campers arrived. It was a young husband and wife, with three small children. Their truck and trailer were very old.

They didn't know how to use the trailer. The trailer belonged to the husband's brother. It was their first time to use the water and electricity at a campground.

Brian put them into Number 7. He showed them how to do the things they needed to do.

"We're here to find work," said the wife. "There isn't any work at all in Indiana. I heard there might be something in Tupelo."

Brian gave them a few places to look for work. He knew from Dr. Singh that the Mississippi State Hospital might need someone. He said, "There are lots of older people here at Trace Park. If you need someone to look after your kids, I'm sure you can find someone."

The young wife thanked him.

Brian visited Nancy most afternoons. There wasn't any change. She lay in bed now. Her eyes were open. But she didn't look at Brian, and she didn't talk. Brian told her, "I saw you in a dream, honey." But she didn't answer.

At night, Brian wanted to sleep. He didn't want to think about what would happen to Nancy. But it was no good. There would be no sleep. He thought about his life with Nancy. It seemed that 25 years went by so fast. Just last year she was fine. She had a job, she laughed. They went to movies and made dinner together. But now all that was changed.

He lay awake, even though it was very late. He turned off his lights and looked out the window. He looked over the dark lake. It was quiet. It was cold tonight, without wind.

Then he saw a light. It was over at Chickasaw Point. He checked the time. It was 2 in the morning. "Who would be out at 2 o'clock in the morning?" he thought. He called the Trace Park office. There was no answer. He left a message. "Hey, this is Brian Longfield. It's about two. I can see a single light at Chickasaw Point. You asked me to call if I saw it. Thanks."

Brian kept looking out his window. Sometimes he saw the

light. Then sometimes he didn't. It was like someone turned the light on, and then turned it off again. Brian wanted to walk over and check. It was such a mystery! But he remembered what the park ranger told him, and he stayed in his trailer. Except for a sky filled with cold stars, it was dark.

After twenty minutes, he could see the car lights of a ranger. The light on Chickasaw Point went out. After another 30 minutes, Brian saw the ranger leave. He didn't see any more lights that night.

CHAPTER EIGHT

The next morning, Brian drove his truck to the Trace Park office. He found Ranger Jack Madison there with another ranger. There was a third man Brian didn't know. They were all looking at something on a table.

"Hi," Brian said to Jack. "I saw you go out to Chickasaw Point last night. Did you find anything?"

"And how," said Ranger Madison. "There were hunters. But they weren't hunting animals." Brian went over to the table where the men were standing. On it, he saw a pile of small, dark stones. No, wait. Those weren't stones. He looked closer. They were all sizes, some small and some larger. And they had different shapes. Some looked like a triangle. Others were rounder. But they all had a sharp point. Some were covered in dirt. But Brian could see that some of the stones were reddish. Others had a pinkish or grayish look. Then he had it. He asked, "Are these Indian arrowheads?"

"Yes," said the third man. "Those are arrowheads. All different kinds. It's amazing."

The four men all looked at the arrowheads.

"So then," said Brian, "where did these come from?"

The man said, "Good question." He held out his hand. Brian shook it.

The man said, "I'm Reggie Buck. I work for the Chickasaw Preserve Museum in Tupelo. Some of these arrowheads are over 1,000 years old. Others are newer, dating from maybe 1450. The new ones are called 'Woodland' arrowheads."

Ranger Jack Madison said, "Reggie here thinks arrowhead hunters have been going out to Chickasaw Point. Whoever it is, they're digging up arrowheads. I think they heard me coming. Then they ran."

"What? Really? Why?" asked Brian.

Reggie Buck said, "Arrowheads are so old. They're small. They're easy to trade. And they're worth a lot of money. You can go on the internet and find lots of places to buy arrowheads. People steal them and then sell them."

"But why Chickasaw Point?" asked Brian.

"Well," said Reggie, "This land was all Chickasaw land a hundred years ago. My people lived here for 400 or 500 years. Chickasaw Point was an Indian village."

"Oh," said Brian. Reggie was an American Indian.

"Yeah," said Reggie. "Anyway, Chickasaw Point was an Indian village for hundreds of years. But some of these arrowheads are much older than the Chickasaws. They were made by people a thousand years ago or more. Chickasaw Point was a good place to

GRETA GORSUCH

live. Those early people may have been Chickasaw, but we don't know. They made the arrowheads by hand, and then tied them to straight pieces of wood. Then they used it as an arrow to hunt animals."

Ranger Madison said, "We think someone is coming to Trace Park and taking the arrowheads. Well, that's got to stop. This is state land now. We'll have some rangers wait at night. We might catch them." He looked at Reggie Buck. "So what should we do with these?" He pointed at the pile of thirty arrowheads.

"Well, I'd love to look at them. But I think we should put them back. We should put them back in the dirt. That's where they belong," said Reggie. "Chickasaw Point is an old, old place. We should enjoy it, not take things away from it."

"Do you know that cell phones don't work out on Chickasaw Point?" asked Brian.

Reggie smiled. Then he laughed. "Well," he said. "Maybe the old Chickasaws don't like cell phones."

The rangers and Brian looked at each other. They couldn't think of anything to say.

CHAPTER NINE

Dr. Singh, Dr. Dheram, and the third man, Mr. Septa, came to fish at Lakeside Campground at sunset. The men drove up in their two cars. They set up four chairs next to the lake. Then they started to fish. The sun was setting red and gold on the water. Brian walked to the lake.

"Here is Mr. Longfield," said Dr. Singh. "We have a chair for you."

Brian laughed, and sat down. "Are you having any luck?"

Dr. Dheram answered, "Well, yes and no. We are catching fish, but we have to throw them back. They are too small to take."

Mr. Septa spoke up, "How are you, Mr. Longfield?"

Brian told them he was fine. He told them about Mr. Felton and his old trailer. He told them about Mrs. Poe and her refrigerator problems. He told them about the old people coming to Mississippi to escape the cold winters. He told them about the young husband and wife looking for work in Tupelo. He told them about the arrowheads. He talked about the Indian village. He told how Reggie Buck took the arrowheads back to Chickasaw Point.

"Ah," said Mr. Septa. "I knew that place was very, very special. It's so quiet. It feels quite peaceful. It's not a bad place. Just a quiet place. And good for fishing!"

They all laughed. They looked across the lake at the dark trees of Chickasaw Point. There were no lights tonight. There was just the sunset behind the trees.

There was a short silence. And then somehow Brian found himself talking about Nancy. He told them how she wouldn't talk. How she didn't look at him. He finally stopped. He didn't know what would happen to Nancy. He didn't want to say what he thought might happen before too long.

The three men listened quietly. They didn't say anything when Brian was finished. Perhaps Dr. Singh and Dr. Dheram knew what might happen. They were doctors.

Dr. Singh said, "Oh, dear, dear. I am so sorry. It is not easy."

Dr. Dheram and Mr. Septa nodded. The four men sat in the growing dark. The lake was silver at their feet. Brian heard a fish splash, close by.

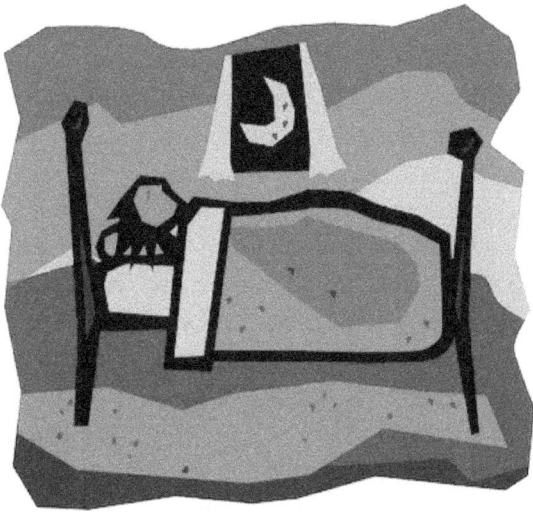

CHAPTER TEN

The next morning, Mrs. Poe from Number 6 stopped by.

"Can I help you?" asked Brian.

"Oh, there's nothing really. I'm just taking a walk. It's warmer this morning, isn't it?" she said.

"That's true," said Brian. It was warmer. It would be a sunny day. It was a good day to be in Mississippi in winter. They talked for a few minutes. The young husband and wife from Indiana found work in Tupelo. Mrs. Poe was watching their children five days a week. "The money will help," she said. "I don't mind telling you."

Brian's cell phone rang. He answered it. He listened. Then he dropped the phone. It just fell from his hand.

"Mr. Longfield!" said Mrs. Poe. "Oh, Mr. Longfield, what is it?" Brian didn't answer.

She said, "We can take my car. Is it Nancy?"

Brian nodded. "It's OK, Mrs. Poe. I can drive myself." Without another word, he got in his truck.

Brian got to the Pontotoc Rose Nursing Home. He found Nancy's room. He looked at her peaceful face. Her eyes were closed. He held her hand. It was still warm. He sat with her until the doctor came.

The doctor told him, "I'm so sorry, Mr. Longfield. She left just an hour ago. We didn't hear anything. We just found her like that."

Brian thanked the doctor. The doctor left. Brian sat with Nancy some more. He thought about the dream he had a few nights ago. Nancy held out her hand in the dream. He was sure now she held an arrowhead in her hand.

Brian looked up. It was a least an hour later. The sunlight in the room looked different. There was nothing left here to do. It was time to go. He had to call Nancy's sister to tell her. He put Nancy's hand down. Then something fell on the floor. It made a loud CLACK.

"What?" said Brian, surprised. "What was that?" He looked on the floor. Nothing. He checked under the bed. Still nothing. Then he looked down. Right by his left foot was a small, dark arrowhead. Brian said again, "What?"

He felt like someone hit him. He couldn't think. He picked up the arrowhead. It was small and cool in his hand. It was clean.

There wasn't any dirt on it. It was a dark color. It had the sharp point at the end. Brian put it in his pocket. He didn't know what else to do.

How did the arrowhead get into Nancy's hand? Where did it come from? Why an arrowhead? What should he do with it now? He couldn't think about that. It was too much to take in.

He left the room to call Nancy's sister.

CHAPTER ELEVEN

A week later, Nancy's sister came. She was younger than Nancy was. She had two kids, a boy and a girl. The boy was ten. The girl was fifteen. Brian never met their father. He was a truck driver, and never home.

The boy, Dale, smiled at Brian. The girl, Willa, said "Hi," and walked away to the lake. No smiles from her.

"Oh well," thought Brian. "She's fifteen." Didn't all fifteen-year-old girls act this way?

Darla, Nancy's sister, wanted to know how Brian was doing.

"I'm OK," said Brian. "Everyone's been nice. I haven't had to cook." It was true. As soon as Mr. Felton, Mrs. Poe, and the other campers found out about Nancy, they came to tell Brian how sorry they were. They brought food every day. The young husband and wife brought coffee every morning. The young wife sat with him before she left for work. Brian was a tea drinker, but he drank her coffee anyway. She told Brian she liked her new job at the hospital. She liked Mississippi. She didn't think she wanted to return to Indiana. "That's good," said Brian.

Darla went to the motel near the park. "Can I leave the kids with you?" she asked. "I'll be back in an hour."

Brian felt sad and tired. But the idea of having two kids with him made him feel better. Each day was so dark and silent. Even Willa seemed like a bright spot, now. Even if she never smiled. The boy, Dale, didn't talk much either. But he smiled at Brian, asked him questions, and then listened to Brian's answers. He showed Brian a book he was reading at school. "We're taking a week out of school right now," he told Brian.

Darla came back with more food. They sat and ate lunch in the warm sunshine. They sat under a large tree. They looked out over the lake. Brian could see the forest on Chickasaw Point.

Ranger Jack Madison stopped by in his car. He asked if Brian needed anything. Brian said no, he was fine. Ranger Madison told him to take care.

Darla and her kids stayed a few more days. They talked about Nancy. Darla asked if Brian would stay in Mississippi. "Don't you want to go back home? After losing Nancy?" she asked.

Brian thought about it. Then he said, "No, I'm OK here for now. The weather is good. I sold our house anyway. I'm not sure what I would go back to. My job here is fine."

Darla, Dale, and Willa waved as they drove away. Then the days seemed to go on without end. Brian felt deeply alone. He felt that from the day Nancy stopped talking. When she wouldn't look at him. As the sun went down, he felt only deep, quiet sadness. He loved sunsets. But he couldn't put his thoughts together tonight. Without Nancy, he didn't know who he was. He didn't know where he should be.

Unable to sleep, Brian walked in the darkness to Chickasaw Point. The moon was out, and he could see enough. He could hear the water in the lake ahead. He heard a bird call. When he got to the lake, he stood and waited.

Then he reached into his pocket. He held out the little arrowhead and felt it in his hand. Then he threw the arrowhead as hard as he could. It splashed into the dark lake. It was silent. Then Brian heard the bird calling again, further away. He heard a big fish splash somewhere. The trees moved in the wind. It seemed like Brian could think again. What he thought was, "Home. This is home."

THE TWO GARCONS

CHAPTER ONE

Jeff Garcon had never been so bored. He was more than bored, he was unhappy and angry, too. Here he was, living in Monroe, Louisiana. Monroe? Louisiana! How did *that* happen? Jeff could not believe it had been two weeks since his family moved away from Wisconsin. It seemed like much longer than that. Jeff was a junior in high school, and a star basketball player. He couldn't be pulled out right now! Basketball season was going to start in less than a month! He didn't want to change schools. He had his friends, both boys and girls. He was in the Spanish club. This was completely wrong! Jeff had plans. And moving to Monroe, Louisiana was *not* part of the plan.

His father, Jackson Garcon, told him, "I know this seems like a bad time for you to leave your old high school. But you'll make new friends. You're a fantastic basketball player. The Monroe Central High School team is really good, I've heard. A lot of college basketball coaches go to their games. I know you want to go to college in Wisconsin. But why not give Louisiana a chance, too? You can choose from more colleges that way."

Jeff answered, "It's not just the basketball, Dad. It's my

friends, my life. I'm in Spanish Club, remember? We're raising money to visit Mexico City, remember? Come on, Dad!"

Jackson Garcon waited. Then he said, "I remember. Look, Jeff. This seems bad now. But in a few months you'll think it's great. This is an important time for your mother. She can start her own doctor's office here. And you know she wants to work in a city like Monroe. And we can be closer to my family here."

Jackson Garcon had been born in Monroe. He had a mother and father, and sisters and brothers living in Monroe. Jeff had cousins living in Monroe. The Garcons were an old family. Everyone in Monroe knew the name Garcon.

Jeff was too unhappy to think about those things. "Yeah, I get it."

But he didn't feel like he wanted to "get it." And so here he was in his bedroom in Monroe, Louisiana. It was just after Christmas. Their new house was full of boxes. His mother, Eve, was a doctor. But she was gone all day. She was busy getting her new office ready. Jeff started school in a few days. It was like a bad dream.

CHAPTER TWO

Four days later, Dr. Eve Hill drove her son Jeff to school. It was his first day. When she married Jackson Garcon, she had kept her own name, Hill. Jackson's mother and father were unhappy about it when Jackson and Eve got married. But now they were happy that Jackson, Eve, and Jeff moved to Monroe.

Dr. Eve Hill stopped the car in front of Monroe Central High School. She looked at the crowds of kids.

"This is beautiful," she said. "The school is older than I thought. Just look at those trees. And the windows are so large." She looked at Jeff. "What are you thinking?"

"I'm thinking how crazy this is," he said.

"Yes, it is kind of crazy," she answered. Jeff looked at her, surprised. "But it's crazy in a good way, too," said Eve Hill. She smiled at her son. "See you at home? You know how to get there from school, right?"

"Yeah," he said, and opened the car door. A wall of noise and laughter came from the kids outside. The front of the school was crowded with boys and girls. They were all sizes, and all shapes. Some were tall, some were short. Some were big, and some were small. And they had every color of skin, from white, to honey, to brown, to black. Eve Hill smiled widely. It was a beautiful sight. A few of the boys, about Jeff's age, looked over and one yelled, "Hey, new guy!" And then Jeff was out of the car. He closed the car door.

Eve Hill waited and thought about all the things she had to do for her new doctor's office. She watched Jeff talk to the group of boys.

It was crazy, she thought. Here she was, opening a doctor's office in the poorest part of Monroe. And she didn't know Louisiana at all. She was from Wisconsin, hundreds of miles to the north.

Louisiana and Wisconsin could not be more different. It wasn't just the weather with Louisiana warm, and Wisconsin so cold and snowy. It was the people who were different. In Louisiana, there were just as many African Americans as there were whites. And just as many Spanish speakers as English speakers.

But Dr. Hill liked the idea of working with so many different kinds of people. She liked the idea of being in a place really new to her. She thought it would be good for Jeff, too. And her husband Jackson now had a chance to grow his window washing business. At the same time, Jeff could get to know the Garcon side of the family better.

Eve Hill thought again of all the things she had to do. She pulled away from the high school.

CHAPTER THREE

Jeff walked in to the school office to find out the times of his classes. He wanted to make sure he was in the right Spanish class.

A short, wide lady with brown skin and glasses asked, "Yes? Can I help you?" Her words were high and soft.

"My name is Jeff Garcon. I'm starting school today. I'm from Wisconsin."

"Ah yes," said Miss Cora Cable. "I'm Cora Cable. I'm the school clerk. I'll help you with your paperwork."

"Thanks, Cora," said Jeff Garcon. Miss Cora Cable looked at Jeff for a long time. She was not smiling. Then Jeff looked down and said, "Thanks, Miss Cable."

Miss Cable smiled and said, "Let's get started. We have your class schedule here. Here is a map of the school. Your lunch time is at 12:30. Be sure to go at that time. You have homeroom in five minutes. Room 277. Do not be late."

"Thank you Miss Cable," said Jeff. He walked out of the office.

"How interesting," said Miss Cora Cable to the empty door. "Now we have *two* Garcons at Monroe Central High School."

Jeff stood at the door of Room 277, his home room. The

school bell rang. He looked at the kids in his home room. And the boys and girls looked at him. There were a few white faces, many brown faces, and a few black faces. A few kids smiled.

One boy, a tall, strong boy with medium-brown skin, did not smile. He looked at Jeff. Jeff looked back. Jeff was tall and strong, too. He didn't know the boy. Maybe he was on the basketball team. He could talk to him about it.

Mr. Howard Sims, the home room teacher said, "Class, we have a second Garcon at Monroe Central High School. Please welcome Jeff Garcon. He's from Wisconsin."

Jeff Garcon thought, "A *second* Garcon?" He didn't think any of his Garcon cousins went to Monroe Central High School. They went to a new high school in another part of Monroe. But there were a lot of Garcons in Monroe.

Jeff looked up as a few students laughed. One short, dark boy said, "Are you sure you're at the right high school?"

Jeff felt strange. He said, "No, this is the right school." A few more students smiled.

There were a few empty desks. Mr. Howard Sims pointed to one of them, "We sit by last name. You can sit behind Corey Garcon."

Jeff went to the desk. Then he saw that he was sitting behind the tall, strong-looking African American boy with the medium brown skin. His hair was dark and curly. It stood straight up and high from his head. The boy turned around and said, "I'm Corey Garcon." Jeff felt his mouth open. His face felt red. He put out his hand and said, "I'm Jeff... uh... Garcon." They shook hands.

Corey Garcon did not smile. But he asked, "You play basketball?"

Jeff answered, "Yeah!"

Corey looked at him and said, "All right." The way he talked, it sounded like *Aaahrai*.

Jeff sat in his seat. He felt strange. He had no idea there were black Garcons. "Well, of course there are," he thought. "This is the United States. We have all kinds of people here. There are white families called 'Smith' and black families called 'Smith.' Why not 'Garcon' too?"

But it felt strange. Jeff's school in Wisconsin didn't have many black students. He didn't have many black friends. When Corey Garcon turned around, Jeff saw he had very light brown eyes. There was even a little bit of gold in his eyes. Jeff had very light brown eyes, too, with light brown hair. And with just a little gold in his eyes, too. But Corey was definitely African American. And Jeff was white-skinned.

"Hmmm…," Jeff thought.

Then homeroom began.

CHAPTER FOUR

Jeff walked to his third-year Spanish class. He really liked the school building. His mother was right. It was an older building. There were some cracks in the walls but everything was painted a rich light color. The dark wood windows were large and tall. They let in the strong Louisiana sunshine. Jeff could hardly believe it was January. In Wisconsin he would be wearing a sweater and a coat. The skies would be full of snow. Here he wore just a t-shirt and jeans.

He moved along with the crowds of boys and girls to his class. Two girls, one pale white and the other medium brown, laughed and talked. They both wore "Monroe Central Swim Team" t-shirts. The second girl turned to Jeff and said, "Are you new here?"

Jeff answered, "Yes. I'm Jeff."

The girl said "Hi. I'm Allysia Cable. She pointed to the first girl, "This is my friend Christyn Baker."

"Hi," said Christyn softly. "Are you going to Spanish?"

"Yeah," said Jeff.

"Well, here it is," said Allysia. "We're in the same class."

"Cool," said Jeff. "Are you related to Miss Cora Cable?"

Allysia answered, "Oh, yes. She's my aunt."

"Oh," said Jeff. "I met her at the school office."

Allysia laughed. "Yes, she's the clerk."

"Wow," said Jeff.

Allysia really laughed then. "Yeah, I know. She can be… well… just be nice to her. She'll warm up."

"No, she won't," laughed Christyn Baker. "No, she won't."

Allysia, Christyn, and Jeff all laughed together.

The three went into class and sat down. The teacher, Mrs. Ada Vasquez, looked up and smiled. She pointed to a desk in the back of the room. Corey Garcon was nearby.

"Oh," thought Jeff. It was still a small shock to see him, and know there was a Garcon at the same school but with a different color skin. But the same light brown eyes. Jeff's mother sometimes said it was the clear brown of a small river in a forest, with little bits of gold. Interesting. Corey was looking at him. He nodded hello and Jeff nodded back.

"Are you guys planning any trips? Do you have a Spanish club?" Jeff asked Alyssia before she went to her seat.

Allysia answered, "Yes. Shhh. We'll talk to Mrs. Vasquez after class."

CHAPTER FIVE

"Silencio!" said Mrs. Vasquez. Mrs. Vasquez spoke in soft Spanish. She told the class about the new student, Jeff Garcon. She asked the students to speak to each other in Spanish. They checked their homework together.

Class went well. Jeff had a great Spanish class in Wisconsin. He felt like he was going to do well in this new Spanish class. He could read and speak well, and fast.

They had a quiz, and the students answered in groups of three and wrote down their group's answers. Jeff's group got eight questions right. But Corey's group got all ten questions right. Mrs. Vasquez and Corey had a conversation in Spanish. Jeff could understand some of it. Mrs. Vasquez asked whether Corey's family would be spending the summer in Mexico again. Corey answered that they would. He and his father's church group would help to build a school in a small town. They would go in June and return in August.

"Wow," thought Jeff. He was more interested in visiting big, old cities like Mexico City. He liked big city life. But the idea of building a school was interesting. If Corey and his dad went to Mexico each summer, no wonder Corey's Spanish was so good.

Mrs. Vasquez then spoke in Spanish to the class. She gave a short lecture. Jeff, Alyssia, Christyn, Corey, and the other students took notes in Spanish. Mrs. Vasquez talked about the history of Spanish speakers in Louisiana. She said that Spanish speakers came to Louisiana in 1716. They wanted land. They wanted to do business with the French speakers in Louisiana. They wanted to build churches and bring the Caddo and Adai Indians into the church. They built a road west from Louisiana and into Mexico. The Caddo and Adai Indians were friendly. The Caddos had lived in the area for almost a thousand years.

The Indians were not interested in joining the Spanish churches. But they did some trade, and the Spanish speakers built a church and other buildings at a place called "Los Adaes" in 1716. It was now a historical park, only an hour southwest of Monroe.

Mrs. Vasquez asked the students what they thought the name "Los Adaes" meant. Jeff answered in Spanish, "For the Adai Indians? 'Los' means 'more than one.' And there was more than… one Adai person?"

"Muy bien," said Mrs. Vasquez. "Very good. The Spanish way to say 'The Adais' is to say 'Los Adaes.' The Spanish simply named their town after the Adai Indians. And we will visit Los Adaes next Friday afternoon. Make sure you tell your mothers and fathers. *Si? Muchas gracias."*

Class was over.

CHAPTER SIX

Jeff got home after school and emailed his best friend in
Wisconsin. The email said:

Hey Eric, first day at school. It was OK. I'm going to try out for
the team next week. I thought I could just join based on my
basketball playing in Wisconsin. But everyone must try out
every year. Even their star players. Wow. That seems hard. But
it'll be OK.

Spanish class is no problem. Do you remember how hard our
teacher was on us? Learning vocabulary and reading and
taking notes in Spanish? Well, it's helping me now. We do a
lot of things in Spanish class here that we do in Wisconsin,
like work in groups. This Friday we're doing to visit a historical
park called Los Adaes. It's pretty old. It's the first Spanish-
speaking town in Louisiana. I never thought of Louisiana
having Spanish speakers. I always thought only French
speakers were here. That's where my name comes from.
Garcon is a French name. I guess my family was French.

The school lunch was weird. We had sweet potato fries! Can you believe that? And something called "jambalaya." It was a kind of thick soup with seafood. Really strong. They don't have hamburgers or salads or regular food. Yuck. I'll have to get used to it.

Mom just got home. I have to go. More soon, see you. Let me know what happens with Lara. Yes, you know which Lara I mean. The one you want to go on a date with? Hmmmm?

Jeff

Jeff got an answer right away. It said:

Shut up about Lara. She's fine, by the way. Everyone wants to know how you like it in deep, dark Louisiana. Everyone talks weird, right?

Too bad about having to try out for basketball. They're crazy not to let you join right away. All of those games you won for us????? Hello??

Got to go. Mike's coming over with his "maybe" new girlfriend, Sayla, and Maria Sanchez, her best friend. Too bad you aren't here to help me with my Spanish. With a name like Sanchez, she has to speak Spanish, right?

Bye, "bro."
Eric

Jeff heard his mother and father open the front door.
"Jeff! Are you here?" called Jackson Garcon.
"Yeah," said Jeff.
"Come on down and help carry this stuff in," called his father.
Jeff sighed and went downstairs to help carry in bags from the

supermarket. The car was also full of bags and boxes from the local Do It Yourself place. There was paint and paintbrushes.

"We have a lot of work to do in your bedroom and the kitchen," said Jackson Garcon. It was true. The house they moved into was old. It was small, and painted white. But, it had beautiful wood floors. Some of the windows were painted blue around the sides. It looked good. There were large trees in front. Jeff didn't know what they were called. In January, they didn't have any leaves.

The house was OK... but it needed work. Some of the walls were cracked. A few of the windows were broken. The kitchen, though, was *really* bad. The windows were dirty. They probably needed to put everything new in there.

"Why did we move to *this* house?" asked Jeff.

His father answered, "This is the best, old part of town. Some of these houses are 150 years old. Your mother wanted to live in a house that looked like Louisiana's past. And it's close to her office, and my business."

"And *how* old is this house?" asked Jeff.

"I would say about 80 years old? I'm not sure," answered Jackson Garcon.

Jeff sighed again. The wind blew a little outside, and the house made a noise like *crack!*

CHAPTER SEVEN

Over dinner, Jeff told his mother and father about his first day at school. After fifteen minutes of non-stop talk, Eve Hill smiled at her husband.

"That's the most I've heard Jeff talk in about two years," she said.

"Mom!" Jeff laughed.

"It's true," she said. "The last two years in Wisconsin we couldn't get you to come to the dinner table. When you came, you had your phone and would just text your friends. So, what's changed?"

Jeff thought about it. "I don't know. It's a new place. It's interesting."

Jeff's mother and father smiled at each other. Jackson Garcon took a huge bite of his hamburger.

"But the most interesting thing was..." Jeff stopped. He waited. He wanted to think about what he wanted to say.

"Yes?" said Jeff's mother.

"There is a black guy in my homeroom with the name Garcon. He's Corey Garcon," said Jeff.

Jeff's father stopped eating. There was a short silence.

"Really?" said Jackson Garcon. He spoke slowly. "That's interesting. Well, there are lots of Garcons here. It's an old name. Your grandfather has all that land outside of Monroe. It's been in the family at least 150 years."

"Yeah?" said Jeff. "But why would there be a black family named Garcon in the same town? You're white. I'm white. Grandfather's white. It's not a common name."

"Yes, and your great-grandfather and great-grandmother, and on back. Anyway, Garcon is not a common name in Wisconsin. But it *is* a common name here in Monroe," said Jackson Garcon.

There was a short silence as the Garcons ate. Finally, Jeff's mother said, "Well, is it possible your family owned Africans to work as slaves on their land?" There was a short silence.

"Yes. It is possible," said Jeff's dad, finally. "That would have been before 1865. They owned a lot of land then. They grew rice, and sugar."

"Then," said Eve Hill, "in 1865 when the war was over, the slaves were set free. Couldn't some of the Garcon slaves have taken the Garcon name?"

"Yes. That is possible, too," said Jackson Garcon.

Jeff felt surprised at this idea. He knew about families in Louisiana owning other human beings. They had been taken away, from Africa. He knew about the big farms in the American south that used slaves. He also knew that slavery ended in 1865 after a long war between the North and the South.

It was one thing to read about it in books. It was another thing to feel it so close to home. He felt strange knowing that his own family might have owned slaves. He felt even stranger knowing that his great-great-great grandfather might have owned Corey Garcon's great-great-great grandfather.

After dinner he helped his father paint his bedroom. The walls were a soft honey color now. While Jeff and his dad painted, they didn't talk much. Jeff had a lot to think about.

CHAPTER EIGHT

The school trip to Los Adaes was interesting. After one week in Monroe, Jeff was happy to leave town. The country outside of Monroe had a lot of trees. Not as many as Wisconsin, of course. But the forests in Louisiana were different. A lot of the trees had greenish gray strings hanging from them. It was beautiful in a strange way.

Jeff was sitting on the school bus with his new friends, Allysia, Christyn, and Corey. He asked Allysia what the greenish gray strings were. She told him, "They're called Spanish moss." Then she smiled and said, "You mean you've never seen Spanish moss before?"

"Maybe in movies!" Jeff laughed.

Jeff looked out the school bus windows. He saw many small white painted houses with a car or truck in front. They passed a few small towns with a gas station and not much more. Then more trees with Spanish moss. Then they came to the Los Adaes historical park.

In Spanish, their teacher told the class that they had one hour before lunch. They could walk around the park. There were two or three park rangers to answer questions. Mrs. Vasquez also told the students she wanted them to read the park signs. All of them had been written in both English and Spanish. "It will be good practice for you to see if you agree with how the signs use Spanish!" she said.

Los Adaes was a huge park. Mostly it was green grass and trees. But Jeff and Corey found some buildings, and signs to read. They learned that Los Adaes had been a town from 1716 to 1770. "That's 54 years," said Corey Garcon. It sounded like *"Thas fif fo yeahs."*

Jeff grinned. Some of his new friends really talked weird.

Then Corey said, "You think *I* sound funny? You should hear what *you* sound like." And then he spoke exactly like Jeff, saying "I've never seen Spanish moss before," and Jeff laughed loudly. It did sound exactly like him, like he was talking fast, and through his nose.

Jeff had never heard Corey make a joke before. In fact, he had never seen Corey smile. He wasn't unfriendly. He was just quiet. He didn't smile much. He watched everything around him. But Jeff could tell when Corey was making a joke.

"Come on," said Jeff, walking to a small building. There was a park ranger there. She talked to them about the building, which was used for business. She told them that the Spanish wanted to do business with both the Indians and the French. They got many things from the Indians and the French, including fur from animals, gold, wood, and food such as fruit and rice. It was a hard time. The French did not want the Spanish there. The French had gotten there first, in 1699.

Jeff wanted to ask the park ranger questions about slaves. But he wanted Corey Garcon to leave first. Jeff felt strange asking the ranger questions about people who may have been Corey's family in the past. Corey showed no signs of leaving, however. Finally, Jeff said to Corey, "Hey, I'll see you back at the bus."

"Uh-huh," said Corey. He didn't move. He looked around the park and up at the trees.

Jeff thought to himself, "Okay, here we go." He asked the park ranger, "Were there African slaves at Los Adaes?" Corey became very quiet. But both Jeff and Corey listened.

The ranger answered, "Not until later. Mostly the Spanish had Indian slaves, both Adai and Caddo. That was in 1722. Then, in 1763 a war ended. The Spanish moved west in 1771, and out of Los Adaes. After that, there were a lot of African slaves working on farms. By 1763, the French had brought 6000 slaves from Africa. The slaves grew sugar and rice."

By then, Allysia and Christyn joined them, and listened, too.

"Oh, no," thought Jeff. But Allysia and Christyn just listened. Finally, the classmates thanked the park ranger. It was time to go back to the school bus. The park ranger told them about some books they could read about early slavery in Louisiana.

CHAPTER NINE

The school bus took them to a restaurant. Everyone had "pulled pork" sandwiches. Jeff had never had this.

"Why do they call it pulled pork?" he asked Allysia.

"Oh, they just cook the pork for a long, long time. They add some sugar. The pork becomes so soft you can just pull it apart. You don't need a to knife to eat it," she said.

It was true. The sandwiches were soft, and delicious. And they had more sweet potato fries to eat. "Of course," thought Jeff.

After lunch, Corey pulled Jeff aside. "Can we talk?" he asked Jeff.

Jeff was quiet for a minute. He thought, "Oh, no." But then he said, "OK. What is it?"

Corey wanted to know if Jeff was planning to try out for the basketball team. Jeff said he wanted to.

"After we get back to school, let's go see the basketball coach," said Corey. "He can tell us when the tryouts are."

"OK," answered Jeff. He waited, and Corey looked at him. Jeff went on, "For a minute, I thought you wanted to talk about my slavery question. You know, to the park ranger?"

"Yeah, I got that," said Corey. Then he didn't say any more.

He looked at Jeff, then away off into the trees, and the hanging Spanish moss.

Finally, Jeff said, "Yeah." He felt something let go inside of him.

They got onto the school bus.

After an hour, they got back to Monroe and to the high school. Corey took Jeff to meet the basketball coach. Coach Hines was a short, quick man. He spoke quickly, and stood straight. Around Coach Hines, Jeff wanted to stand up straight, too.

"I'm Jeff Garcon," he said. "I moved here from Wisconsin a few weeks ago. I played basketball."

"Oh, yes?" said Coach Hines. "Good enough. Tryouts are tomorrow. Be here at 8 a.m. Do... not... be... late." He gave them both a hard look.

"Yes, sir," said Corey Garcon.

"Yes, sir," said Jeff Garcon.

"Hmm. Hmm. You can practice a little now," said Coach Hines. He threw a basketball to them.

Corey and Jeff went out to the basketball floor. They threw the ball and ran for about an hour. Corey was a fast runner. He got past Jeff a few times, and made baskets. But Jeff had fast hands. He got a few baskets away from Corey. Coach Hines watched for awhile.

A few other boys joined them. One of them was the short,

dark-skinned boy from Jeff's Spanish class. He laughed. "You still here? Are you sure you're in the right school?" he asked.

Jeff shot back, "Are you sure you're on the right basketball team?"

Coach Hines said, his voice hard, "No one's on this basketball team yet. Got it?"

They all played for another hour. The short boy was really, really fast. He got balls away from everyone. He made at least two baskets.

Then Coach Hines came out and told them, "That's enough. Go on home."

By then it was dark outside. It was winter, and it got dark early. It didn't feel so warm after it got dark.

"Where do you live?" asked Jeff. Corey told him. It was only five minutes away from Jeff's house. Jeff called his mother. He asked, "Can I bring a friend home for dinner? It's Corey."

She answered, "Of course. We have lots of food. When will you be here?"

Jeff told her they would be home in a few minutes. They got to the Garcon's house. Jackson Garcon was just getting home. He looked at the two boys and said, "Hey there."

Jeff introduced Corey, saying, "This is Corey Garcon. He's in my Spanish class."

After a very short silence, Jackson Garcon put his hand out. He said, "I'm Jeff's dad. I'm Jackson Garcon." They shook hands.

"Nice to meet you," said Corey. It sounded like *Nisa meetcha*.

"Come on inside. I'm hungry," Jackson Garcon said. They all went inside.

As Corey left to walk home, he said, "Don't let Ethan get to you. He's the short kid in our Spanish class. He's all right. He just talks before he thinks."

"No worries," said Jeff. "See you tomorrow at the tryouts."

"All right," said Corey. He nodded goodbye.

CHAPTER ELEVEN

The basketball team tryouts started at 8 a.m., just like Coach Hinds said. Corey and Jeff were both there. Ethan was there, talking and moving fast. About twenty boys were there. Some were white, some had dark skin. There were two smaller boys there, with light brown skin. Jeff could hear them speaking Spanish to each other. "Well, well," he thought. "Spanish speakers in Louisiana." The idea no longer surprised him. He knew about towns like Los Adaes now.

Coach Hines came out and told them to get started on a basketball game, with six boys on each side. They would play until the best team won, up to five points. Then the winning team would go up against a new team.

The basketball tryouts were hard. Everyone wanted to be on the basketball team. Everyone played hard. Jeff and Corey were put on two different teams. Then they had to play against each other. Ethan, who was on Corey's team, ran fast at Jeff. Jeff went over hard, and for a minute, he could not get up.

Corey Garcon came over and put his hand down. He said, "Get up. Get up. Let's play." Jeff got up, and then, they played.

BOOKS IN THIS SERIES

American Chapters books by Greta Gorsuch

- *The Bee Creek Blues & Meridian*
- *Lights at Chickasaw Point & The Two Garcons*
- *Living at Trace*
- *Summer in Cimarron & Lunch at the Dixie Diner*
- *The Storm*

www.ingramcontent.com/pod-product-compliance
Lightning Source LLC
Chambersburg PA
CBHW021144020426
42331CB00005B/888